GW00865208

The Purrfect Little Cat Book

A Catalogue of my life--With a little help from my owner

by

Treacle Pelling

Bloomington, IN Milton Keynes, UK

authorHOUSE®

AuthorHouse™
1663 Liberty Drive, Suite 200
Bloomington, IN 47403
www.authorhouse.com
Phone: 1-800-839-8640

AuthorHouse™ UK Ltd.
500 Avebury Boulevard
Central Milton Keynes, MK9 2BE
www.authorhouse.co.uk
Phone: 08001974150

First published by AuthorHouse 1/26/2007

ISBN: 978-1-4259-6372-9 (sc)

Printed in the United States of America
Bloomington, Indiana

This book is printed on acid-free paper.

Acknowledgements

My Thanks to the following:-

Extracts from the book Cats (Home Reference Library)
by Paul McGreevy MRCVS Ph.D. , B. Vsc.

Extracts from the book The Little Tortoiseshell Cat Book by David Taylor BVMS, FRCVS and Elizabeth Martyn

Verse – Faith, Fact and Feeling by Rev. Pamela Russell

Mr. David Gladstone – Trustee – SANE

Owners of cats mentioned in this book. Anyone else mentioned.

Editor of Park Magazine

Cats Protection

Barbara Hesketh for typing manuscript

Publishers: Authorhouse of Milton Keynes

Anyone else who has helped with the manuscript

Gosport Resource Centre Stoke Road-for helping with text and advice

Table Of Contents

My Lovely Cat

Treacle is my lovely cat,
In the evening she sits on the mat,
She gives me a look as if to say –
Don't just sit there, I want to play.

Treacle has a lovely fur, black, ginger and white,
When I give her food, she thinks –
'That's alright'.
She laps up the water in her bowl –
She enjoys it so much, I know by her purr.

Treacle is my lovely cat –
Every day she runs around the flat –
On the chair or on the bed –
She does not mind, as long as she is fed.

When my friend came for the day
Treacle still wanted to play
And when we had 'tea' –
She thought 'What about me!'
Treacle is a lovely cat, but can also
be a rascal when she wants to.
She rolls around, climbs up high and gets
Herself in a stew.
She lays on her back with her legs in the air
She does not care.

If I am trying to write a letter –
She sits on the paper to show off –
And thinks 'That's better!'

Treacle to me is like a good friend
I know our bond will never end.

Bridget Pelling - 2004

Chapter One

Me as a Kitten

I was born round about the middle of May, somewhere between the 15th to 19th. May's a nice month to be born in and last May, the year 2005, I was 3 and so far I have had a party the nearest Sunday to my birthday.

I remember my 1st birthday party, we had ginger bread men, but one had a leg missing so I thought he should go to the hospital where Bridget used to work and have a plaster put on it. The three children who lived next door came to that party but they went to the Emerald Isle to see the Irish cats. I like my parties but had never seen so many people before and at my 3rd party, I was a little shy, so I hid behind the curtain on the kitchen window sill till they all went home – then I came out and it was just me and Bridget again. I had some money, some cards and lots of food given to me which was the best because I like my food (Bridget does too, but don't tell anyone about that, she likes to go anywhere where there is free food). If we both put on weight, it's our own faults!

I was 6 weeks old when Bridget got me, a friend knew a lady in a nearby road who had me and my brothers and sisters. I was chosen because I was the loveliest of us all and I am called Treacle – because

I AM

SWEET

My middle name is Lovely because

I AM

And one day Bridget wrote a poem about me – called –

MY LOVELY CAT

This poem is in the front of this book, please read it –

I LIKE ATTENTION!

I am a 'tabby', the proper name for my breed is a British Shorthair, and I am glad that I am British because I would not like to be French (they eat snails there!). I don't like them. I am a very Patriotic cat anyway.

We are the oldest of the British breeds and brought to Britain by the Romans.

Our name comes from an Indian word – a part of old Baghdad known as Attabiya. Patterned silk called 'tabbi' came from the west there.

We did not get to the USA until 1964, so we are fairly new over there. I would not want to live in America far too big for my liking.

I'm a patched tabby – this is because I have tortoiseshell markings on me too. Us cats are all over the world, even on the Isle of Man (humans again!) and the <u>paw</u> cats there have got no tails, it must be very difficult for them to sit down. I'm glad I've got my <u>tail</u>, if I did not have it I would not be able to write this book and I've got a <u>tale</u> to tell you here.

My colours are black and white and ginger and I have a large black spot on my chest and white above it and a ginger part below it, but my prettiest part is my underneath.

When I roll on my back with my legs in the air I show off my underside and I am in my element then!

Sometimes I am called Marmalade. I suppose there are cats called Marmalade but Marmalade is not as sweet as Treacle is, and Treacle is also called Golden Syrup – being golden it also means I'm precious.

Bridget told me she once knew a cat called Marmite because he was all black like Marmite is and a dog called Honey (she was sweet too, but not as sweet as me!)

So I'm Treacle and there was Honey and Marmite, but so long as none of us were called 'peanut butter', Bridget and I don't like peanut butter. If we were all there together we could <u>spread</u> ourselves around.

Bridget's sister said the markings on my paws look like I've got socks on, but I need something on them to keep them warm don't I.

I told you I've got brothers and sisters, but I only know about one of them and that's my sister Willow, she's got a nice name too, but I hope she does not weep a lot. And I've been told that Willow had some kittens, so that makes me Aunty Treacle and I like being an Aunty.

By the way, I cannot have any kittens because I've had that '<u>cat-snip</u>', even though I was going to be an indoor cat and not meet any other ones, they still said I should have it done. But I did not like having that thing round my head for six weeks to stop me from scratching myself and pulling the stitches out, but when Bridget tells me one of her jokes and I laugh at it I get the stitches anyway! I don't suppose you knew that cats can laugh, well we can you know, we cats are very clever, in fact so clever that the ancient Egyptians used to worship us. I like being worshipped. We cats are also intelligent and I am very intelligent like Bridget and owners are supposed to be like their pets.

If I had been able to have kittens, I would have been a Queen, that's what we are called when we have our young – I would have liked to have been a Queen because as I said I like being worshipped, it's so that I can show off more. But never mind, I am a Royal Cat anyway. (I will tell you why in another chapter)

Ever since I came to this flat, I've always been a little madam – Bridget calls me that sometimes, but I like it. Very often, she says to me- "oh you are lovely" and I say - 'meow' – yes, I know I am.

Incidentally, I wonder why male cats aren't called Kings when they become fathers; it just goes to show us females have got the upper hand!

When Bridget was a little girl and living in a place called Woking, she had a longhaired male cat. Male cats are called Tom but his name was Twinkle, he was a nice cat and a rascal like me, and Bridget and her sister Janet would sing a song to him;- it was called -'Twinkle, twinkle little star – how I wonder who you are', but I would have known who he was if I had been there because we cats can tell one another a mile off!

When Bridget had me I also became a very lucky cat because I came to a good home where I would stay for the rest of my life, cats who are indoor cats like me live longer and people who have cats for therapy like me are supposed to live longer too, I hope we both do.

As a kitten I was always very good at using my litter tray and learned to use it before I came to live here which was helpful to Bridget. I was a good girl. I will tell you more about my ablutions later on.

I used to have a cat bed and slept in that curled up in the bedroom but now I sleep on the bed.

Because I don't go out much my claws get very long and I have always had one that is extra long. I use the furniture to sharpen them and ignore that scratching post, it's because I am a rascal and I don't like that word 'NO'.

I got up to more mischief when I was young in this flat and would explore everywhere. I remember once when I was quite young I hurt myself on something and had a scratch on my neck, so Bridget contacted her friend who lives near and she came round. I was on the kitchen table and they bathed it with warm salt water and it soon got better.

That's what you get when you become inquisitive – that's a tongue twister, but by the time I have finished this book my tongue will have twisted around a few more long words. But there is one short word that I don't like, and that's that word- 'NO!.......AGAIN!'

Chapter Two

I am a mischievous cat

I am a mischievous cat, I always have been and even though some might think it is unnatural for me to be an indoor cat – I like it.

I have comfort, fresh water, (not that dirty puddle water) special indoor cat food to keep me healthy and best of all, I can curl up on a chair or on the settee and go to sleep (we cats sleep about 16 hours a day and in the winter it is even better to curl up in front of the fire).

I like Bridget's flat. There are five big rooms and I know where all the nooks and crannies are and each room has something different in for me to play with – I like the kitchen window sill but I get told off because I jump up on the table first to look out of the window, but I know I must not jump up on the kitchen table, but there's only and old shed out the back anyway, so it's not a very nice view in any case.

Talking of cases, there are two on top of the wardrobe in the bedroom, one green and one blue. I used to jump up on the portable TV on the table next to the wardrobe and sit on the blue one, but I don't do that so much now, but I've left my mark up there – hairs everywhere – moulting it's called. Bridget used to say to me "what do you want to sit on that old rough case for when there is a big bed here with your own blanket on," but I would ignore that, funny aren't I.

About the bed – I sit on the bottom of it when Bridget is in it – a big lump – but when she goes away and Yvonne comes in to check me during the daytime – I still sleep on the bed at night, but I miss the lump! I know Bridget misses me too, but I know she has to have a break now and again, and I have to lump it!

When Yvonne comes, she is very good at looking after me – she gives me treats and makes sure I have enough water and food and that my litter tray is OK.

I like to play with my toys more and get up to even more mischief when Bridget is not around to see me. I spy on her when she is here and she thinks I am not looking at her but I am and I sometimes hide from her making her wonder where I am.

My most favourite toy is a green/red ball with an orange stripe on it. It has a rattle inside and when Bridget throws it along the hall I chase after it, I would play with it all day if I had my way – I do enjoy it.

Ever since I was a kitten, one of my other favourite things has been thin plastic straws. Bridget brought them in a tub from a nearby superstore called Waitrose, and I am glad they sell them – I like to play with them with my paws, toss them in the air and put them in my mouth and chew them, I play with them on the bed as well.

The bedroom window sill is another place I like to be, but when the window is open the blind has to stay down – otherwise I would be out there. The other morning, I had my head sticking right outside between the blind – but Bridget walked in on me and told me off. "If that blind had not been down you would have been out there and lost," she said. When I am sitting on that window sill in the sitting room, the window cannot be opened any more than 2 inches or else I would be out there too, in the winter it is closed all the time. Bridget said she is not going to take the risk of me getting out and getting lost.

One day when I was very naughty Bridget told me that I was up to my <u>antics</u> again. But I don't like <u>ants</u>

and I don't like <u>ticks</u>, so I had better stop getting up to those antics in this flat!

I don't want to get out really – no food or comfort, no fights with other cats, no germs – oh! it's a good life indoors although I have got that microchip thing inside me in case – it has a number on it so that if I did get out and got lost someone would know who I belonged to and contact Bridget. She would be very upset if I got lost, so would I.

Back to that microchip thing, it did not really hurt me – just a stun, but if I had got lost they would have to scan me to find the number, so I would then have a <u>cat</u> scan.

As for those chips – that's what humans have with fish, I like fish – a nice bit of cod or some pilchards – very posh!

That number I have in me – well there's 2 0's and a 7 = 007 – James Bond!. But I'm even better – I'm Premium Bond (ha, ha) – most superior and that's that Bond we've got.

Back to the flat – another room I like is the dining room because thats got a mat in it that I like sitting on – sometimes I close my eyes to have a '<u>cat-nap</u>'

With all these rooms around – I don't like it when that hoover goes round them – horrid noise, but I like the flat better when it's untidy anyway, there's more things around and boxes for me to sit in. 'Bridget's got another computer chair and I soon made it my home.

Then there's that room called a bathroom – I'm supposed to stay out of there but as I am usually disobedient anyway,I like to go in there, but Bridget says – "can't I have any privacy in here, its alright for you, you don't like it if you're using your litter tray and I'm there do you?" Well she's right, you know, because I'm very particular about my ablutions (big word, I think it comes from the Navy that Bridget used to be in). I always have been since I was a kitten, and I do look up to see if she is watching me, we cats have to keep ourselves clean, so I am always licking and grooming myself – so long as I don't get any of those hair-ball things.

My claws are quite long and need to be cut regularly, there is a scratching post with a ball on in the sitting room, but I ignore it and prefer the furniture – although I get told off – you can't take me anywhere can you!

Every so often I have to go to the claw clipping shop but I don't like getting into that cat carrier and I kick up a fuss every time I have to get in there and sometimes Diana has to come down from the flat above and help Bridget get me in there – tempted by food again of course! I am getting very heavy for Bridget to carry me now and she has to keep changing hands, good job its not too far to go, only a short distance. I suppose soon she will have to try and find someone who can come to the flat to cut my claws, but it will cost her more – I'm very expensive but worth it! I remember once Yvonne tried to cut my claws but she put a horrid green towel round me and I went berserk and snarled my teeth, I did not like it at all. But the next time I saw her I was all lovey, dovey towards her again.

When I have to go to see that nice lady vet, Yvonne takes us, but its that carrier again, she has to pick me up and put me in there – we get there in the end and

13

on time (I don't like being late) I'm not keen on car journeys, but I know that the sooner I get there and get it over with the sooner I get back to food again and familiar surroundings. As we are going along, there are round things in the middle of the road that glow in the night - they are called <u>cats</u> eyes – they are nothing like my eyes – they are pretty and mine glow all the time. I don't know why they don't call them dog's ears instead and then they could hear the traffic coming.!

That vet's place is new – it used to be where humans went when they weren't well, but now it's where us animals go when we are not feeling very well or need to be checked over, like I am every year. I don't like those injections I have to have to stop me from getting illnesses, but I know I have got to have them. Bridget told me she does not like having to go to that man called a dentist to have her teeth checked, but she still has to go.

Inside that vets surgery it is very nice, but it says that we cats must go on one side and those dogs must go on the other side. But I thought what about all our other animal friends – those rabbits, guinea-pigs, hamsters and others. I suppose they have to go on the side of us cats – they can get ill too, but those dogs want to be on their own – they think they are better than cats and other pets – but they are not – we cats are!

I like being a pet and being petted and I like Bridget's company, we talk to one another – I like her talking to me – except when she tells me off – it's called an affinity – what we have got and I like affinity.

I sulk when Bridget goes out – all the time until she comes back. In the morning when she gets up I try and stop her from going out, but she says -"If you don't let me go out I cannot do my shopping, then I cannot buy your food," so I think – well I had better let her go then – I've got to have my food!

I do play up in the morning and I'm also very vocal and soon let Bridget know if I don't like anything. She shuts me in one of the rooms for a few minutes – she says she has to see if that post has come, but I am more important in the mornings than that post and she should pay more attention to me!

Next time she went out – I thought up another trick and when she tied her laces up I undid them again - I thought she can't go outside without her shoes on, she does not like getting her feet wet (like me, I don't like getting my paws wet).

I'm a little young lady and a little madam – always have been – I would walk around the flat with my head up and my tail up 'here I am I thought' – I've come to stay and must have notice taken of me – even though I don't come in contact with many people – I still like to show off when I can! But Bridget said she's the boss in the flat not me and I've got to learn to do as I'm told, but I don't like the thought of that very much.

Two of my favourite games are 'I spy' and 'hide and seek', but most of all I like playing with those straws and that ball in the hallway – it is long and 'L' shaped – so lots of room for me to run in – only when Bridget's at home though.

One day she walked into that kitchen to get something out of the cupboard underneath the sink – so I jumped in quick before she had a chance to close it. Bridget said- "come on out, you are a rascal," so out I came along with a pink round thing with a hole in the middle. "It's a toilet roll" she said, but I thought I did not know that toilets could roll, I thought they were those big round things in the bathrooms, oh! well, I'm young yet and still got a lot to learn.

As for that jumping I do, I jump up on the ledges and other places if I can, but I must not jump up on that kitchen table, its out of bounds like that oven.

Sometimes I jump if there is a noise or bang outside or next door that scares me, but otherwise I jump when I am happy. I must be like those big animals that jump a lot called Kangaroos in that very big country called Australia, but I would not like it there anyway – too hot for me and I would try and jump back to England if I had half the chance – I would miss Bridget and my comfort and food and everything else here, as I said before I'm an English Cat and I'm proud of it.

When Bridget's friends came for her party they brought her a long thing. It is called a doorstop, but it was six cats all lined up, with a large one at the end and five small ones. Of course, I knew they were not real, although they looked real – they could not say 'meow' like me and if they had been real I would have chased them all round the flat. I don't know why they were called a doorstop, because if we had all been running round the flat we would not be able to be stopped going into each room through the doors would wc?!

On the wall in the hallway, is one of Bridget's favourite poems – it is called <u>IF</u> – part of it says; -

'If you can meet with Triumph and Disaster'
And treat those two impostors just the same!

Bridget has had a lot of Triumph and Disaster in her life, and I don't like it when she gets upset because that upsets me too. That poem was written by a Mr.Rudyard Kipling – but I thought that Mr. Kipling made exceedingly good cakes!

When Bridget had some trouble at the place she used to work in in this town, it upset her so much and went on for over two years, but she is <u>purr</u>sistent and got there in the end. I wanted to go and tell them to stop 'pussy footing' around with her. It was <u>cat</u>astrophic what they did to her – <u>paw</u> thing! Oh it did make my <u>whiskers</u> bristle!

Back to us cats again – Bridget told me once that in that Naval place she used to work in, there was a cat. That Naval place had a post office in it then and that cat used to sit on the counter in the Post Office. His name was Odd Job and he was a very handy cat to have around.

When Bridget and I am here together we often have a <u>chat</u> and I'm very vocal and let her know what I think – it's that Bond we have again, and I have also got my own little character as we all have.

One evening I was sitting in the hallway and out of the corner of my <u>eye</u> I saw Bridget standing near me looking at a picture on the wall and thought-'<u>eye</u>,

<u>eye</u>-' she should be looking at <u>me</u> instead- Im' a pretty picture!

Bridget told me that in a country that is on the other side of the world called New Zealand she has a sister called Jan who has a cat- he was at her house when she moved there. He has put on weight since Jan moved in! He has a funny name and is called 'Fluffy Bum' but I'm fluffy all over and those poor Manx cats need fluff on their rears don't they!

Bridget told me that it took her 30 years to trace Jan in New Zealand. I thought '30 years' – if you had given me a sheet of that tracing paper and a pencil I could have gone over to that place and put that paper over her and traced her in 30 minutes! She is long winded in doing anything, but as I said, she is also <u>purr</u>sisent and always gets there in the end. I think there's no point in giving up on anything is there and she is also like us cats because we always fall on our feet but when anything ever happens to Bridget she has always fallen on her feet but in another way of course.

In New Zealand where Bridget's sister lives, there are a lot of those creatures called sheep – they follow one another around and have wool for their coats not fur like us cats, but I like playing with balls of wool and it is made into lots of different colours. On the settee where I sit, I have my own woollen knitted blanket with different coloured squares on it – mainly those blue and red colours. It was knitted by a nice lady who was not very well in the other smaller hospital in the town. But one day it was not there and in its place was another one that I did not like – I wondered where the other one was and I did not sit on it. All of a sudden it was back again a few days later – I was glad to have it back – I don't like change, but Bridget told me it had to be 'washed' so it went in the white square thing with a round window in the front that keeps going round and round and makes me feel 'dizzy'. When I do that moulting, I leave my hairs all over the place, those dogs do as well when they moult but we cats keep ourselves much cleaner by grooming and licking ourselves all the time.

When Bridget goes away for a few days, I do miss her but Yvonne comes and sometimes Diana who lives in the flat above looks after me when she just goes out for the day and she gives Diana something to say thank you for looking after me. But when Bridget gets back into the flat, she says it's in a mess, I thought well I must be like those army soldiers – they live in a 'mess' too. She used to do ironing for people in the flat and have a long white flat thing on legs that she would put up to do that ironing on, but she told me to keep away from that iron or I might burn myself – I don't want to do that. I've been told I must also keep away from all those things called leads, switches and flexes or I might get a shock. I don't want to get a shock so they are all out of bounds and I get a shock when I hear loud noises that make me jump, I don't like it so Bridget strokes me and gives me a kiss and I feel much better. I like it when she gives me a kiss but she says my nose is wet, but when my nose is wet it means I am healthy.

I like it when she does that ironing though because there are a lot of those things around the flat to put the clothes on – they are called hangers, but when the people come to collect the clothes, I have not got anything to play with that hang down like sleeves on shirts – so I say to them 'hang about'- I don't want you to take them home because they will not be hanging on the door knobs in the flat for me to knock down', I did that once and Bridget gave me such a telling off she said- "you must not knock them down because they do not belong to me and I do not want you to get those hairs of yours all over them or I will not get any money from the people I have ironed them for, so I thought I had better not do it. I don't want Bridget not to get any money or else she won't be able to go to those shops to buy my food and I <u>must</u> have my food.

Bridget's very lucky at winning raffle prizes and one evening she went to a social and brought some of those raffle tickets. One of them came out of the hat and she won a bread maker but it was new and she did not want it, so she sold it because she 'kneaded the dough' (literally!) ha, ha! She does not like not having much money now.

Bridget has to go to those shops often and that means she has to go out and leave me – she looks out of that big window in the dining room to see if that rain is coming down or that sun is shining and I think <u>weather</u> it rains or <u>weather</u> it doesn't she still has to go, she needs food too.

There was one of those dogs next door and sometimes he was vocal and I could hear him barking – I didn't like it when he barked and I am glad that there was a wall between us, but if he thought I was going to pay any attention to him then he was barking up the wrong tree!

About those trees that they have outside - they have <u>bark</u> on them. My favourite cat litter comes from a tree, it does smell nice, pine its called, I don't miss those trees because sometimes us cats get stuck up them and cant get down again. I don't want that – they would have to get those firemen out to get on their ladders to rescue me. We cats have got nine lives, and I told you about one of mine when I hurt myself as a kitten – so I have eight lives left and I am glad I have – I will live longer – hoorah!

Back to the flat again and that kitchen room, when we wake up Bridget walks in there and says- I'm going to put the kettle on, well I often think it must be very heavy and uncomfortable for her to have it on, especially when that hot 'steam stuff' comes out of the top. Polly used to put that kettle on, but Suki took it off again and I don't blame her for taking it off – it must have been very heavy for her to have it on too.

Then Bridget goes and puts some things called cornflakes in a dish to have with milk and that's what interests me and I stand there and wait till she gives some to me too, then I lap it up. Bridget once brought me some special cat's milk but I did not like it. I prefer the cow's milk that humans have, but she told me off for wasting her money. Anyway, I only have the milk in the morning and the rest of the time I have fresh water.

At night time my food dish and water dish go in the bedroom and Bridget told me in the morning that once she woke in the night and heard a noise, I expect is was my tongue lapping the water up because once I get going drinking the water it's nearly all gone, or the noise she heard may have been when I knocked over the waste paper bin.

21

I expect Bridget thinks how I manage to see in the dark when she turns the light off. Well, I don't eat carrots, I don't like them – it's just that our eyes adjust to light and dark. Now then there's one other thing about that kitchen place and a little green ball thing which is called a pea. One day one of them fell out of a bag of them that Bridget had in a big white box thing called a freezer. I chased it all round the floor and enjoyed it – but oh it was cold on my paws! Next to that big white thing called a freezer, is another big white square thing with four black round things on the top. One morning I jumped on it, but I got such a telling off – "if that had been switched on you would have burnt your paws young lady and then you would have known all about it." I was naughty and that thing is now out of bounds, out of bounds!

Over the other side of the kitchen is yet another white square thing with a large round thing in the front on a door. One day it was making a noise so I sat in front of it to find out why, but it was going round and round, it was making me so dizzy I stopped looking at it.

Another place in the kitchen I like to be is up high on the toaster which has a cover over it and is not used so it stays on top of the kitchen cupboard and when I'm up there I can look down on Bridget in the kitchen and check up on her – she says "what are you doing up there, come on down and stop spying on me".

My favourite place in the kitchen is by the back door because that is where I sit if I want to go out, so long as I've got my collar on, the double lead can go on to take me out the back ,when I sit there I am in anticipation

– waiting so Bridget says – but sometimes when I'm out there – I don't like it then and want to come back in again – Aren't I strange!!

My favourite room is the one that is called a sitting room. I call it the comfort room. Here I spend a lot of time, it has big windows, so I sit on top of the cabinet in front of them and look out – it helps to pass some of the time away. If Bridget's been out I sit there until she comes back and when I hear her put the key in the door I am ready to greet her. I rub myself against her legs to let her know I'm there – it's that affinity again.

Sometimes when she's had a bath and got no shoes and socks on – I rub my head on her feet, but she starts to laugh – she says it tickles!

When I was two I had a birthday card from Bridget's friend. It had a black and white cat on the front like me – he was sitting looking out of the window and underneath were the words neighbourhood watch!

When I sit on my cushion at the window and look out, I watch that neighbourhood and the <u>purr</u>imeter- I like to see who's walking along the road and which cats go up and down, and I keep my eye on them all.

If anyone tries to break into the flat he would not get very far when I'm here. I would soon let everyone know so that they could get help and that police force out to check. I am a better guard in this flat than any dog would be, I would hiss at them and then they would not come near this flat again and that is <u>cat</u>egorical!

One day Bridget had two people come to see her, but I don't like it when there are visitors, because I don't have any attention, so I jumped up on the arm of the chair and looked the man in the face – as if to say -who are you – I have not seen you before!

Sometimes I do wish I was out of that window, but then when I see that water falling from the sky I'm glad I'm not out there – I don't like getting my paws wet.

This flat fortunately is on the ground floor. I would not like to go up those things called stairs. That means it has that back yard that I mentioned about earlier on, but I only have my collar on from March to September, then it comes off for the rest of the year – 'hooray'!

When I do get out the back, I have a sniff around, but pooh! that drain smells – I stay away from it, but I do go round the side of that shed and look at those weeds, when Bridget pulls them up, they come back again. Then I go up the other end and sniff around there too, it's a pity there is not grass, only hard concrete, but it is covered with that green stuff called moss. I do miss grass to eat sometimes but Bridget makes sure she brings some in from outside to put in a bowl for me to eat so that I don't miss out. Sometimes there's a breeze and I like cool air on me when I'm out there, but when that rain comes again I'm back indoors in safety and comfort once more.

I don't like noise and sounds – they scare me and make me jump, and one day a big long thing in the sky went over us called a plane, it made such a noise, I was glad when it had gone. Of course its <u>plane</u>, its not as pretty as I am! There's another loud noise I heard one evening when I was trying to nod off on the settee, it made my ears stick up and I did not like it at all – humans call it thunder, but I call it a big bang.

Talking of big bangs, there's a whole week in November when a lot of bangs and sparks go off and I don't like it – it scares me – it makes my ears go up. It's called Bonfire night, but to me it's Bonfire week and if I had my way I would get rid of it in a flash!

I was telling you about this here sitting room. Well it's got lots of things in it I like and I get up to a lot of mischief in that room. There's a black square thing with a screen called a TV I think and when its switched on a coloured picture appears on it, but I don't watch it, it only interests me when the cat food adverts come on then I sit there and lick my lips.

There's another square box with a screen on it in that room, called a monitor with a long thing under it with letters and numbers on. A lot of people have them nowadays and they are called computers. Information can be found on them (a lot about cats too) and other things. Nowadays all these gadgets are called mod-cons but out of all of them I like this one the best because there is another part of it called a <u>mouse</u> – it's not supposed to be a real one but if it was I would chase it all round the flat. I like the thought of mice and one day Bridget changed a little arrow on that computer thing and it turned into a black and white cat just like me and I thought to myself – '<u>yahoo</u> – I'm on that monitor too!' Now I can get those <u>fe-mails</u> and not those <u>emails</u>!

Because I'm an indoor cat, I don't bring mice or those birds inside, so I help keep the flat cleaner. 'Bridget does not want them inside,' she said, oh well, I can still think about them all day can't I. If I see one of those noisy flies come in, I chase it too, I don't like

25

them, neither does Bridget – she said they spread those germs around everywhere.

In that sitting room there are a lot of chairs and sometimes when Bridget sits in one I jump upon her lap (I am then a lap cat) but just as I start to get comfortable, she says I must get off because she has to go to the bathroom, so then I go and sit outside the door and wait for her to come out again.

Once she went into that bathroom and water was sprayed all over her, she told me it was to keep her clean, but I would not like getting my paws wet, let alone any other part of my body.

Back to that sitting room again, I like all those cupboards, anything to poke my nose in or anywhere up high and I'm in my element yet again. I like being in my element, but that kettle that Bridget puts on has got one too. In that sitting room I like lying on my back rolling on that thing on the floor called a carpet and sharpening my claws on those chairs and that settee, but oh I get told off again because I have ignored that scratching post. I get upon that TV and that shelf above the fireplace and knock things off onto that carpet and Bridget calls me a rascal once more.

I like lying on my back with my legs up although it is not very elegant. I do it to show off my shiny fur and one day Bridget had a small black square thing with a switch on. She pointed it at me and pressed the switch, she did it about five times and every time was different and I remember she did it to me when I was a kitten too. They are called 'snaps' and they all come out as nice pictures of me. All of these snaps are in a book called an album and I have got one all to myself and if it gets full I'll have another one all to myself all the time I am growing up. I like these pictures of me as I am very photogenic (another big word) and in that bedroom there is a big shiny thing that reflects – it's called a 'mirror'. I sat on the bed and looked at it one day and saw this cat, and I thought Bridget had got another one until I looked again and then I realised it was <u>ME</u> I was looking at. Then I thought 'yes' I am lovely aren't I, there's no other cat like me, definitely not in this town, Bridget likes me and I like her and we are going to stay together forever – no other cat will come between us.

Bridget once said to me – I have never known a cat like you in all my life, but there has never been a cat like me in all her life. I'm the best!

There's a thing in this town called a local paper and Bridget told me that she read in that paper about a thing called a pet competition. She wanted to enter and send one of those 'snaps' taken of me to come out on top again. She chose the best one of me out of that album. I was sitting upon the cupboard in the sitting room showing off my pretty front. When she told me I was very excited – I wanted to win because the prize was a years' supply of food and a picture of me to go on the wall. (I would like that), I was looking forward to it and waiting for the day to come. She took the snap of me to the local office and got it there in time. Then when the day came she looked in the paper and that snap of me was <u>NOT THERE</u>!

So Bridget contacted the local office to find out why and they told her that they did send my snap to the other office called HQ but they did not receive it, there was a muddle up.

They did say they were very sorry but when Bridget told me I was so upset and disappointed, I sat on that mat in the dining room and I yelped and yelped for over half an hour. Then Bridget told me that to make up for it they will come themselves to take a special snap of me next year, when they have that competition again. That made me feel better – I shall be special next year.

That competition was for all pets, so some of those snaps were of those dogs and some were of other animals called rabbits, hamsters and parrots. There are such a lot of us creatures of all different types on this earth but to me us cats are the best. A lot of famous people have had us cats as pets – that is because we are companions to humans and some of us are for 'therapy'. I like being a therapy cat – I get stroked more and I like being stroked, it makes me purr more. When I am brushed I purr more too, when Bridget's Mum came to stay she brushed my fur when I was sitting on the bed – I did like it – I purred and purred then.

I'm Treacle – a cat – but I'm a pet too. Bridget told me that since she has been in this flat she has had other pets. When she came to this town and flat from London when she was in the Navy, she came with a creature called a goldfish in a plastic bag of water. She held him in that bag of water sitting in the front of the van all that way and when she arrived at the flat she put him in a bowl of water until she got a glass bowl for him. She said his name was Goldie and he was a tough old thing because he lived a long time and there was one of those snails in with him to keep the water clean. That snail was lucky living with Goldie and not living in France, if he did I don't think he would have lasted long – they eat them there!

Years after Goldie went Bridget got three more of those goldfish and they were called Scales, Gills and Fins – which were good names for them, but they lived in a tank (not the type the Army have). They had no snails in with them and did not live as long as Goldie did. Those goldfish must be precious too if they have gold on them, but Goldie had some silver on him as well, so he was extra special.

If I had been around when all those fish were here, I would have been very tempted, but I would have been told off and told to stay away from them. Then Bridget told me about a blue bird she was given one year for her birthday (Bridget has been in this flat many years) the bird was called a budgie and its name was Beauty (a bird called Beauty – no way – I'm the beautiful one). Every day Bridget would let him come out of his cage to fly around the flat (to get that exercise like I have when I run around the flat) but he would perch on the lampshades and would not get back in the cage again – a bit like me – would not do as he was told – naughty bird. Bridget had him about five years then he went.

If I'd been in this flat when those fish and that bird were here I don't know what I would have done – because I like to be in charge and it's me that is more important than them and that temptation would have come upon me again.

I expect those fish and that bird liked living in this flat with Bridget, she looks after me so well and I like living here, every day is an adventure and I like to get up to that mischief.

One day Bridget went to help at one of those things called a rummage sale in a church hall. Her friend had a pink T-shirt for her and on the front of it was- 'owner of the worlds' cutest cat!' That's me, oh I am lovely. Bridget has a lot of those T-Shirts but I don't know why they are called T-Shirts, she drinks many cups of tea during the day and she usually has a jumper on, so why aren't her jumpers called T jumpers too.

There are a lot of my friends who live in this road and Bridget's friends a few houses away have a cat called Poppy and Bridget's got a photo of her too that her owners gave her one day. Poppy is a pretty name to have and it means remembrance and I often remember her and all my other friends and wonder how they are getting on.

One day Bridget came in and had to give me some bad news. She told me that she had heard that my mother had gone. I was so sad and I rubbed my face up against hers for comfort. Then I thought of my brothers and sisters and knew that my sister Willow would be weeping even more.

Then soon after that happened Bridget gave me some good news to cheer me up. She told me that she is one of those agents for a <u>cata</u>logue firm (this book is one of those <u>cata</u>logues of my life). The firm is called Park and they also have a magazine called Parklife and they wanted photos of pets, so Bridget sent one to them of me and they accepted it. They told her it would go in the March edition and I was very excited. But when it was printed they called me a male cat, never mind, it was one of those mistakes.But I like being in the Park. Famous at last!

Diana's sister once had a black and white cat called Liquorice, but Liquorice went without having any kittens, but I wish she did have some, a lot of different ones to leave behind because then they would have been Liquorice Allsorts.

I like it when I'm here in the flat with Bridget on our own – I like to protect her – she needs to be protected too.

Bridget had some trouble with her computer and took it to a shop for them to fix it, it had one of those viruses on it. After a week or so they informed her that the viruses had gone and would not come back, so she went in a taxi to collect it and they charged her a lot of money. But when she got it home and connected again that virus was still on it and nothing was changed. So she contacted the shop again and she was told a man would come round to fix it and it would be a free visit and she would not have to pay again. But the man was not very nice, did not do anything and was going to charge Bridget another £25. She was cross because she was told by the shop it was a free visit and would not pay him, so she sent him away with a flea in his ear. Now I hope that flea stays in his ear and wriggles so that he will know not to do it to anyone else. It made me so cross too, I felt like whacking him for doing that to Bridget, but I managed to stop myself. He won't come again as long as I'm in this flat.

Sometimes there is a ring in the flat and Bridget picks up a long white thing with buttons and numbers on – it's called a phone – and she starts talking into it.

I turn my back on her when she does that – no attention to me and I've <u>got</u> to have the attention, every room she goes in I follow her – even in that bathroom.

That phone rings a lot – even when I'm here on my own – but Bridget has not taught me how to answer it yet – I expect it answers back like I do when she tells me not to do something.

Once she was talking into that phone in the sitting room and she said it went faint (perhaps it was not feeling very well) so she had to go into the bedroom to use the one in there. I said its phoney – take it back and ask for another one!

When Bridget comes in she checks to see who has spoken to her when she has not been here, she is very popular some days - with lots of messages, but still not as popular as me!

I don't like it when Bridget goes out and I sulk until she comes back. Sometimes she comes in, says- "Hello Treacle-" then she is off somewhere again and I give her such a look as if to say- "where do you think you are going-" and when she is back- I give her another look as if to say- "where do you think you have been." One morning when she was getting ready to go out and leave me – I did not want her to go so I gave her a whack and thought that'll stop her, but I know when Bridget is going out – its when she puts that coat on and puts some fresh water in my drinking bowl – once I get going with that water its non stop, but the only way she can get out of the doors is to entice me with some food by putting it in my food bowl and waiting for me to start eating then she shuts the sitting room door behind her and puts the latch across so that she can get out of her flat – she has to do this because if I was not shut in that sitting room when she went out I would be all over the flat and make that mess again. I would also run out into the hallway when her flat door was open and probably go up those stairs to see Diana, but its that front door of the whole house that must stay closed or I would be out there in that nasty road – I would not like that at all – I don't want to get out and go missing like some of my cat friends do – so that front door must stay closed because of that temptation of mine again.

That food I get is special dried food for cats like me who stay indoors – its very crunchy and tasty and it keeps my teeth clean, that's so that I do not have to have a brush put in my mouth to brush them – the only brush I like is the one that I'm brushed with all over my body and tail – I like it so much it makes me purr and meow.

One day Bridget's Mum came back from a holiday with a present – it was a plastic mat to go on the floor to put my feeding bowls on and it said on it- 'come and get it' -so now 'I go and get it' and every time there is food around I make sure I get it – I like my food!

When I'm in that room when Bridget is out, she puts on that radio thing for me to listen to – we both like listening to classic FM – very posh!, but when I'm on my own and listening to it I jump up on that settee and lay my head back on the arm of it and the music is very soothing – I almost drop off to sleep, I like all the music except when <u>Bach</u> comes on – it reminds me of dogs! When Handel's water music comes on I have to then get up and use my litter tray, but very soon I'm nodding off again – this is a good life!

33

On one of the chairs in the sitting room is a large black plastic bag with lots of strips of shredded paper in – letters that Bridget no longer wanted.

I love that shredded paper – Bridget has something that's shredded for her breakfast when she does not have those cornflakes – she said it's called shredded wheat – too tough for me. That shredded paper in that bag is very comfortable and I love sitting in it, curled up and sometimes I nod off in it and go right to the bottom. When I do that sometimes she cannot find me in the flat until she sees the lump in the bag but I like playing tricks on her.

I told you I am a special cat, well I must be a famous cat too. This is because I must be in a film – a little actress – Bridget said when I am in the flat with her I cling to her, so I must be in that cling-film she has in the kitchen, but she told me its what's used to wrap food in not a film you would watch on that telly or at the cinema, but I can dream about it – can't I!

One evening I was <u>cat</u>-napping on that settee and Bridget thought I was asleep but I wasn't. She was talking to someone on that phone and I was eavesdropping. I heard her say that she was soon going to a quiz evening at one of the churches. Then she said they were going to have 'bangers and mash' to eat. I thought – well that's strange because I thought those bangers were those firework things that made those loud noises I don't like during that bonfire week! I did not know that you can eat them, but then I discovered that they are really 'sausages' and I started to lick my lips. But when Bridget got home from that quiz she did not say anything about those sausages, which is just as well because if she had told me about them she would not have heard the last from me because when it comes to anything to do with food I'm very vocal.

Once I was told that Ive got a mind of my own , but I would rather have my own mind than another cats mind. I had to <u>make up</u> my mind to write this book, but actually it is not <u>made up</u> – its true!

Now I am coming to the end of this chapter, the longest one. Bridget does everything by the book and so do I, so please <u>buy</u> the book. I have not needed <u>a gent</u> when Bridget has helped me. I hope you enjoy reading it, as I have enjoyed writing it and telling you about my life so far – aged 3. I have had a good and eventful life so far and in 10 years time when I am 13, I hope to write another book about the rest of my life up until then. 13 is supposed to be an unlucky number, but with a bit of luck this book would have raised a lot of money in the meantime. I hope that I will still be here and living with Bridget wherever she will be. She has helped me to write this book and I thank her.

Some of my friends have lived to be older than 13, but then they have not written books. But I thought Bridget has written 3 books and I want to be a little authoress too.

Now I have been told to think of a <u>re</u>-<u>tail</u> price for my book, I have got to be <u>re</u>-<u>tailed</u> or I won't be able to write another book and Ive got a <u>tale</u> to tell you again, so please wait for it, I'm so cxcited.

I also want to go <u>fur</u>ther –a- <u>field</u> in a few years time and hope there will be lots of <u>fields</u> all over the place with my <u>fur</u> in them !

LOOK OUT- HERE I COME!

Thank you again

Treacle

Chapter Three

I am a faithful cat

I was going to call this chapter 'I am a Religious cat' then I was going to change it again to 'I am a Christian cat'. Then I put on my cat thinking cap and decided to call it - 'I am a Faithful Cat'. This is because some humans cannot accept the words religious or Christian and both can mean different things to different people, so I thought it best to use the word <u>Faith</u> instead. Faithful can also mean loyal and trustworthy too, and I am toward Bridget.

Bridget has a faith and I'm glad she has a faith. She told me it has kept her going through 'thick and thin' - when she's been upset or anxious and glad and happy, and we both want her to keep this faith for the rest of her life.

When she got me at 6 weeks old, she gave me some of her faith too. She said it is God and his Son who gives her this faith – two very nice beings who she knows exists.

Some people think she is strange having this faith – but that is because they do not understand it – but it inspires her and as long as she is inspired I am glad.

She said this <u>Faith</u> goes with <u>Hope</u> and <u>Charity</u>, so I <u>Hope</u> that you will have enough <u>Faith</u> in me and Bridget writing this book to buy one when it is finished so that the money can go to <u>Charity</u>.

Bridget goes to two Churches, and one of them in a place nearby called Lee is called St. Faiths. It is named after a young girl who lived in that country called France a long time ago in 304 AD.

The Church of St. Faiths has a newsletter – it is called Faith Works. I know that Bridget's faith has worked for her, so I am sure my faith will work for me too.

Here's a little rhyme that both of us like, it's about faith and also about fact and feeling too, which to me are very important too;

'Three men were walking on a wall,'
'Feeling, Faith and Fact'
Feeling got an awful fall
And Faith was taken aback
Faith was so close to Feeling, he fell too -
But Fact remained and pulled Faith up
And that brought Feeling too

It's a fact that I like feeling nice too.

Bridget said that God and his Son gave me to her and we both thank Them because we like one another and both like Them.

I believe there is a God because if there isn't I would not have those Waitrose straws and that ball to play with. Bridget said they are a Godsend, so if God sent them to me, He must exist or else I would not have them would I .

When I was ten weeks old she said she was going to Christen me. She was Christened when she was four weeks old in a big round stone thing called a font with warm water in it.

When I was Christened it was different. I was sitting on the dressing table in the bedroom. Bridget had a small round bowl called a chalice that she brought back from that place she went to many years ago called the Holy Land where God and His Son lived. - it was made of olive wood. She put a little drop of water in it and then Blessed it. Then she put her finger into it and made a little cross on my forehead and said

'I baptise you Treacle Lovely Pelling –
in the name of the Father and of the Son and
of the Holy Spirit'
'Amen'.

Then a warm feeling went right through my body – I liked it.

That Father and that Son and that Holy Spirit are going to keep both of us safe forevermore. Then Bridget gave me a kiss and I liked that too. Usually humans get a candle given to them when they are Christened but cats can't have those – so we get kisses instead.

I wanted the cat that was then upstairs – Tabby – to come down and be my Godmother but she was nowhere to be seen but I knew I had God's presence with me anyway.

I also know that God exists because He blesses me. When it's time for us to go to bed - Bridget says to me "Good night God Bless" and I jump up on the bed and we both go off to sleep.

Bridget blesses me too – one day she was dusting with that feather duster and a bit of that 'fluff stuff' got up my nose and it made me sneeze – so Bridget said "Bless you."

I like being Blessed. Bridget told me that God and His Son live in a place called Heaven now and one day we are all going to join Him.

It's a very nice peaceful place – Heaven is – where there is no sorrow or unhappiness, and it lasts forever and ever. Bridget also told me that God and His Son have their own book written about them – a very big book in two parts with lots of chapters in. It's called 'The Bible' and lots of people read it and lots of people don't read it.

Animals are mentioned in the Bible and in the first part there is a story about a man called Noah who had an ark full of all of us animals that lived on the earth.

He thought that we were all so special that he wanted to save us all from a very big flood. He and His family and each pair of us animals stayed on that ark for forty days – then old Noah let out one of his doves and one of his ravens to give the all clear – he was a very good sailor – was old Noah - I wonder if he had been in the Navy, and then a rainbow came in the sky and old Noah knew that from then onwards everything was going to be alright and he let all the animals out again to dry land.

In the second part of that Bible, there are lots of animals mentioned. There were camels, birds and lots and lots of those fish – some of God's Sons friends were fishermen and in that stable in Bethlehem, where God's Son was born, there were oxen, sheep, donkeys and in the whole Bible there were lots of other creatures even an asp in that Garden of Eden!

When I was fourteen months old - St. Thomas' Church held a pet service and asked anyone to take photos and prayers to the service to go on a large board in front of the altar. Bridget took a photo of me, and wrote a prayer – here it is:-

'Dear Father'

Thank you for giving me my lovely cat, Treacle -
She has given me so much companionship
and love for fourteen months and may she
continue to do so for as long as she lives,
through our Lord Jesus Christ –
Amen

All the owners were standing at the altar with the priest when the prayers were said and I'm glad that Bridget thanked God for me. There were photos of other cats, dogs, rabbits, birds and even a horse!

The priest told them all that he thought it best to have the photos of their pets because if they had tried to actually take their pets to the Church, there may have been a few of the smaller animals ending up inside the bigger ones and that would not have been very good. I would not have done anything like that in a Church because I am a good cat. Bridget goes to Church on Sundays and when she comes home I say to her- 'What do you do when you go to Church'. She told me there are a lot of hymns there – I said 'Hymns' – aren't there any '<u>Hers</u>' too? – only men again, but she said that they aren't those type of '<u>Hims</u>'– it means lots of verses like poems with music put to them and they sing them. She said that the best <u>hymns</u> that have been written, have been written by (hers) – women! One of mine and Bridget's favourite hymns was written by a woman and it's all about animals and nature. It's called;-

'All things Bright and Beautiful, All creatures great and small'.

————————

I'm Bright and I'm Beautiful and I'm Great – but those mice are small – but God loves us all.

Sometimes there is a hymn sung called;-

'

'We plough the fields and scatter – the good seed on the land'.

That's a nature one too.

There was a Saint who loved and looked after all the animals, he lived a long time ago in a country called Italy and his name was Francis - he was very poor but would give some of his food to the animals so that they had enough to eat too - he was a very nice man.

Bridget told me that at Church they all say a prayer called - 'The Lords Prayer' and she said it to me. When she said the part of it that says- 'Lead us not into Temptation' - it reminded me of those goldfish that Bridget used to have and how tempted I would have been if I had been around then.

Once when Bridget went to a Church service she said they gave her a little drop of wine and some bread, but I would have liked a little drop of water or milk instead. As for that bread, I would not have had it, but I am glad Bridget did – she needs all the bread she can get. That's because she told me that she now lives on the breadline and she does not like living on the breadline and I don't like her to either, it means she does not have as much money as she used to, less money for her – less food for me!

Many years ago Bridget used to study all about God and the Church. It's called Theology and it interests me too.

When Bridget gets back from Church we sit down and discuss other things that are said during the service. One Sunday she told me that they talk a lot about peace in the Church. During the service she told me that they said- "The peace of God which passes all understanding"- I did not understand what this meant, so I said to Bridget "which <u>piece</u> of God is it that passes all understanding"- God has lots of <u>pieces</u> because He is very big and if any of His <u>pieces</u> pass that understanding – we will not have any and we all need understanding.

So now I've come to the end of this chapter and will say what they say at the end of those prayers;-
Amen (men – yet again!)

Really the word Amen means 'let it be so' which is an Aramaic word from the language that God's Son spoke when He was alive and living in that Holy Land – but lots of people who have that faith believe He is still alive today and that part of Him is that Holy Spirit which is forever.

So now it's <u>God Bless</u> and <u>Yours Faithfully</u> –

Treacle

Chapter Four

I am the Royal Cat

Bridget used to be a Nurse in the Royal Navy. She was in for fourteen years- that was a long time.

At the Palace there is a nice Princess – she is the Patron of the Naval Nurses.

At Christmas Bridget sent her a Christmas card, a poem she wrote about me and some photos of me. Bridget had a nice letter back from the Colonel who helps the Princess. She liked my photos and <u>ME.</u>

Now I am the Royal Cat and from now onwards I am the Right Honourable <u>TREACLE PELLING.</u>

I like being the Royal Cat – it means I can show off even more now.

There are some of those dogs called Corgis at the Palace, but I would not take any notice of them because I have got the upper hand, or should I say the upper paw! The Princess came to the <u>Cat</u>hedral on a Tuesday in November. She came for a Remembrance Service for all the Naval Nurses who have gone before us.

Bridget told me she was going to see the Princess and I wanted to go too, but she said I couldn't (I had forgotten to get my ticket). So I told her to put those photos of me in her handbag and from then onwards to carry them everywhere she goes because I don't like being left out of anything!

Every time she comes in now, I say to her - "Well where ever it is you have been to, did you show them the photos of me, I hope you did, because I am very important now!" If I had been at the <u>Cat</u>hedral I would have done a little curtsy to the Princess and she would have shaken my paw – I would have liked that. I asked

Bridget to let the Colonel know that I wanted to go too.

Bridget told me that next time she puts my collar back on she will attach a crimson bow to it. Now I sit on a union jack flag on the sofa!

There are not many cats in the Country with a poem about them and some photos of them at the Palace.

I would now like some of my photos to go to No.10 Downing Street for the PM to see - He would like me too.

And there is one place I <u>have</u> to get to;-

The White House......

To see

Mr. President

Then me –

Little Miss Treacle

Will have Conquered

<u>The World!</u>

Chapter Five

My Favourite Places and Things

MY FAVOURITE PLACES

<u>PUR</u>BROOK – This is a place near Portsmouth

<u>CAT</u>ISFIELD – This place is not too far away where there is a <u>cat</u> in a <u>field</u>

<u>FISH</u>BOURNE – near Chichester – where Bridget was born –

then to the Isle of Wight

on the

<u>CAT</u>AMARAN

─────

<u>On the Isle of Wight is</u> -

<u>FRESHWATER-</u> This reminds me of my bowl of fresh water.

<u>COWS</u> – These are those animals that give us that milk that I like a little of in the morning

<u>RYDE</u> – This place reminds me of going for a ride – but not when I have to go in a car to the vets

54

<u>FISH</u>BOURNE – Another one on the island – not where Bridget was born

All these fish around, it makes me feel hungry – tempted again!

<u>THE NEEDLES</u> – These are sharp, but knitting needles are not sharp and they were used by those nice ladies to knit that blanket I like to sit on on the settee.

<u>MY FAVOURITE THINGS ARE:-</u>

Those Waitrose plastic straws and that green and pink ball with the bell in are two of my favourite things. I like playing with them.

_____

Topcat – is one of my favourite films – I'm the <u>Topcat </u>of Hampshire!

_____

I like Tom and Jerry – it is a funny cartoon. Bridget went to a Christmas Fayre and on one of the stalls were 6 hooks to hang on the wall. She brought them all for a £1.

They were Tom and Jerry hooks, but all of them were of Tom - the cat. So I had some Christmas presents of my own to give to my friends and now I'm hooked on them!

There are some films that have cats in which are not very nice – so I won't say anything about them.

I like the book;-

'<u>Puss</u> in Boots' -

but I don't know how a <u>puss</u> got into <u>Boots</u>, it's a chemist shop where Bridget goes to buy her soap and toothpaste.

—————

I like Bridget's jokes – she makes me laugh – did you know that cats can laugh – well we can and I often do.

—————

Bridget has written two joke books – one for the Dr Barnados Homes and the other one for the NCH – so please buy them to help save the children – they need protecting too.

—————

Any cardboard box or black plastic bag with shredded paper in are my favourite things.

—————

Sometimes when the radio is on a lady says- 'We are going to <u>paws</u> for thought'. I like listening to that - my <u>paws</u> have been helping me to <u>think</u> what to write in this book.

Chapter Six

My Friends

Fluffy Bum
My Friend
In
New Zealand

I have written this <u>cat</u>alogue of my life to help raise money from donations for the sale of this book for the Cats Protection.

These are my friends, so please help them all:-

Willow	Fletch	Tigga
Bronte	Cody	Tabs
Tabby	Fluffy Bum	Pepsi
Poppy	Stripey	Max
Fletcher	Pebbles	Suki 3
Alan	Jess	Oscar
Tufty	Suki 1	Sadie
Bourneville	Cocoa	Charlie
Mitzi	Suki 2	Murphy
Pogo	Misty	Salem
Casper		

And all others

Thank you very much

Love Treacle

Chapter Seven

Tortoiseshell

Facts, Myths and Feline Information

Compiled by
Treacle,

with a little bit added.

For centuries, the tortoiseshell cat was a great puzzle to naturalists and even nowadays, producing a tortoiseshell kitten is really more a matter of chance than experienced kitten planning. The various complexities of feline genetics governing colour mean that almost all tortoiseshell cats are female. Every now and then, through a genetic hiccup, a male cat appears.

- Anyone in the home who suffered from warts could be cured by stroking the afflicted area with the tip of a tortoiseshell cats tail.

- Households in Scotland welcomed them in, believing that they brought good health to all the family.

- Tortoiseshells are thought to be lucky in many parts of the world. In England tortoiseshells bring good luck to their owners and anyone playing with a tortoiseshell kitten may even be given the gift of second sight.

- Bridget played with me when I was a kitten so now she has second and third sight, that's because I was extra lucky.

- The tortoiseshell variety of cat has always been more common in the Orient than elsewhere, and probably originated in Asia Minor. Its scarcity also makes it a lucky talisman. In Japan they are also a prized rarity, considered to possess certain magical powers.

George Stubbs, the eighteenth century British artist best known for painting horses, produced his only study in oils of a cat in a painting of a charming tortoiseshell and white kitten, which belonged to a friend. The only other time a cat appeared in his paintings was when he featured one alongside a horse known as Godolphin Arabian. The cat had been the horse's lifelong friend. When the horse died, his faithful companion kept watch by the body, grief stricken, until he too went. At the end of the nineteenth century, he turned out feline pictures by the hundred. His Parisian studio was particularly well – located for the artist to observe French street cats.

The gifted and reclusive artist Gwen John, eclipsed by her larger than life brother Augustus, relied heavily on her pet tortoiseshell cat for company. She sketched the cat who, although female, was named Edgar Quinet, after the street in Paris where she lived and was heartbroken when one day her pet strayed away from home and did not return.

Bridget would be heartbroken if she lost me, that's why I don't go out, to stop that from happening.

The British Tortoiseshell shorthair – like me are robust, chunky and rounded (I'm around all the time). A favourite domestic cat and home companion. We are both companions to one another.

I am the <u>A</u>. <u>B</u>. <u>C</u>. cat too.

A is for the affinity we have
B is for that Bond I told you about.
C is for the companionship.

(and D is for Dogs – so I wont mention them !)

We tortoiseshell cats develop a taste for luxury (you bet!) and warm pillows for our owners. I like to warm Bridgets pillow – I purr and purr when I am sleeping next to her head. Two bedheads!

Now I will tell you about my star sign. (There are some humans who do not believe in star signs or horoscopes, but I have stars in my eyes anyway!.) I told you I was born in the middle of May, so that means I was born under the star sign of Taurus (an old bull), they are those animals like cows that that milk comes from that I like a drop of in the morning.

A Taurus cat is always purring and is happiest when asleep on the bed. (This is me to a T, and that's that tea again).

We Taurean cats love our food, and I remember telling you about this before in this book. I've even dreamt about it when Bridget's not been able to give me any.

We are placid and easy-going (if I had anywhere to go I would get there easily!). When we are angered we react fiercely, I whacked Bridget once when I was upset, but I did not mean it and afterwards I was sorry and all lovey-dovey towards her again.

Bridget's birth sign is Virgo and they create homes that Taurean cats love, so that must be one of those coincidences again, but I believe it was <u>fate</u> that brought us together in the first place. That must be because Bridget likes going to those <u>fetes</u>, she told me that she can pick up a lot of those bargains at <u>fetes</u>.

Now we are back to that weather again, and also that Navy that Bridget used to be in. Those sailors used to be on ships, and although Bridget was a nurse in the Navy and not a sailor, she got me for companion<u>ship</u>, so there is the connection!

A lot of ships used to have cats on, sometimes we were called mascots, and if ever a ship was in trouble the cat was always the first to be saved. Good.

When the weather changes we cats can predict it.

Sometimes I scratch behind my ears, but I haven't got an itch, it means that that rain is in the offing. ("I wonder where the offing is?")

When I warm my back in front of the fire – Jack Frost is then on his way, but we do not want him to come, so I will ask him to stay away.

When I am sleeping with my paws over my nose, it means that Gale is coming. I have nothing against Gale, but when she comes, she brings those storms with her, so she had better go and stay with Jack Frost instead.

So that's the end of those forecasts and now I hope that all your futures will be happy ones.

I hope that you have found this last chapter an interesting one and informative and once again – Thank you very much.

Love Treacle

Just as you thought I had finished, I have now got one of those <u>PS's</u> for you:-

<u>Here it is</u> –

Although I am not yet four I am a very clever cat and learning all the time. I have written this book in my own way (with only a smidgen of help from

Bridget.) That's a funny word isn't it. Some of the words and phrases I have repeated, but that does not matter, I wanted to emphasise them, and some words have been underlined. These words have two meanings and I have done this on <u>purp</u>ose, this is because when words are wrested from the true sense – it is called – <u>cat</u>achresis.

Goodbye and miaow

Printed in Great Britain
by Amazon